MW00879129

The Electoral College vs A National Popular Vote

Electing the President and Vice President of the United States

David C. Wilson

Copyright © 2020 by David C. Wilson

All Rights Reserved.

No part of this book may be reproduced, stored in a retrieval system, or transmitted in any form, or by any means, electronic, mechanical, photocopying, recording, or otherwise, without prior permission of the author.

Library of Congress Control Number: 2020902932

ISBN: 9798614307967

This book may be purchased in bulk for promotional, educational, or business use. This may be purchased as print on demand from most major retailers who sell books.

First Edition 2020

Cover and interior design by David C. Wilson

Printed in the United States of America.

DEDICATION

Willie Wilson Sr.
1910–1959

This book is dedicated to the loving memory of my late father, Willie Wilson Sr. Your courage, heroic efforts, and faith during an extremely challenging period in American history and your gallant determination to vote will always be appreciated and remembered. Although you were repeatedly denied—and ultimately never given—the right to vote, you, nevertheless, fought a just and courageous fight until the bitter end.

Author and Publisher, David C. Wilson

Preface

Despite a long history of success since the US Constitution was ratified more than 225 years ago, the often-misunderstand Electoral College[1] is still being debated versus a popular vote relative to its representation of the people's wishes in electing the president of the United States of America. The Electoral College provision was ratified under Article II, Section 1, Clause 2 (Modified by the 12th Amendment in 1804) of the US Constitution, which covers the election of the US president and vice president. Additionally, Article IV, Section 4 of the US Constitution guarantees every state a republican form of government.

The book is broken down into chapters that can each be considered a synopsis of the Electoral College process. Chapter One—Introduction provides an overview of the Electoral College. Chapter Two—Methods of Equal Proportions explains the methodology for selecting the number of House seats every decade because the number of electors in the Electoral College is based on the number of House seats plus two senators from every state. Chapter Three—The Power of Electors by State describes with examples the power that small and large states have in voting with or without the Electoral College process. Chapter Four—Evidence of Proportionality describes with examples the proportionality of population relative to the Electoral College. Chapter 5—The Electoral College Process describes and lays out the Electoral College process in accordance with the US Constitution. And finally, Chapter 6—Summary reviews the advantages of the Electoral College versus a national popular vote.

I use proportionality often throughout the book. In mathematics, proportionality means that two quantities or variables are related directly or indirectly—that is, if one changes in size, so does the other. Therefore, proportionality in this book means that each state is represented fairly and statistically in the Electoral College relative to its population and voting power.

I feel I have made a powerful case in this book—mathematically and graphically—for keeping the Electoral College rather than switching to a nationwide popular vote to elect the US president and vice president. This method is not only fair but also compatible with the US republican form of government.

[1] The Associated Press Stylebook and dictionaries agree that Electoral College should be capitalized, and words and phrases such as elector and electoral votes should not be capitalized. This book follows the Associated Press Stylebook guide by capitalizing *Electoral College*.

Contents

List of Figures and Tables

List of Figures

///

List of Tables

Chapter 1

Introduction

1.1 Background

The concept of proportionality is used as a measure of fairness and justice in statutory interpretation processes. Therefore, as defined in the preface of this book, proportionality means that each state is represented fairly and proportionate in the Electoral College relative to its population. Hence, proportionality is measured by voting power and the proportional relation between the population, electors, and voting power of the individual voter. These measures are discussed in Chapters 3 and 4 of this book.

The Electoral College can be considered a weighted voting process in that every state uses a winner-take-all process to award its electoral votes, except Maine and Nebraska, which use a modified split system. The winner-take-all method means that the candidate receiving a simple majority of the popular vote receives all the state's electoral votes. Thus, a president and vice president are elected indirectly by popular vote. This subsequently gives each state a voice in electing a president and vice president of the United States. The Electoral College process enables each state to have a voice because it forces all candidates to put together a winning coalition relative to the slate of electors from each state. Therefore, to achieve this objective, candidates are forced to consider smaller and larger states—therefore, giving a voice to all states.

This book provides strong reasoning as to the proportionality and fairness of the current Electoral College process, which is used instead of a popular vote method to elect the US president and vice president. Originally, the framers of the constitution discussed electing the president by popular

1.1 Background, *cont.*

vote, Congress, or the Electoral College method. In the end, however, they decided on the Electoral College process. It also has checks and balances.

The Electoral College's number of electors primarily relies on the size of each state's delegation to Congress; therefore, the Electoral College cannot be discussed before understanding the House of Representatives apportionment process. The size of each delegation to the House of Representatives was established under Article 1, Section 2, Clause 2 of the US Constitution, which requires that states be represented in the House of Representatives in accordance with their populations. The criteria are that the number of representatives shall not exceed one for every 30,000 residents, but each state shall have at least one representative. Currently, the total membership of the House of Representatives is 441 members. There are 435 representatives from the 50 states. The number was fixed at 435 representatives by Congress in 1911. However, there are five nonvoting delegates, representing the District of Columbia and the US territories of Guam, the US Virgin Islands, the Commonwealth of the Northern Mariana Islands, and American Samoa. In addition to the House delegation, Article I, Section 3, Clause 1 established that each state will have two senators. The 17th Amendment modified these criteria and further defined the terms and election of senators, which was ratified on April 4, 1913.

1.2 Establishment of the Electoral College

The Electoral College process was established under Article II, Section 1, Clause 3 of the US Constitution. Clause 3 was clarified and modified with the 12th Amendment to the US Constitution and ratified on June 15, 1804. The Electoral College is a process whereby the US president and vice president are elected, and it is made up of electors from each state and the District of Columbia. The number of electors from each state is based on the combined number of representatives and senators from that state. The method of equal proportions ensures proportionality of the electors' count. In addition, the 23rd Amendment extended the right to vote in a presidential election to citizens residing in the District of Columbia by deeming the district electors in the Electoral College as though they were a state. This amendment was ratified by the states on March 29, 1961.

For example, if a state has five representatives, plus the fixed number of

1.2 Establishment of the Electoral College, *cont.*

two senators, that state is entitled to seven electors, or votes. The number of electors from the 50 states totals 535. The 1964 presidential election was the first presidential election that the District of Columbia participated in, bringing the total number of electors to 538.

Over the years, there has been much criticism of the Electoral College process and debate on whether electing a president should be done by popular vote. Each state is a sovereign state operating under the laws of the US Constitution (Article IV, Section 4 guarantees every state a republican form of government). Using the popular vote method, however, means a large state such as California, with 14 million votes cast in 2016, could overwhelm smaller states by muzzling their voices. The Electoral College process is governed by the Office of the Federal Registrar.

Preamble

Figure 1.2.1: Preamble—"We the People of the United States, in Order to form a more perfect Union, establish Justice, insure domestic Tranquility, provide for the common defense, promote the general Welfare, and secure the Blessings of Liberty to ourselves and our Posterity, do ordain and establish this Constitution for the United States of America."

Chapter 2

The Method of Equal Proportions

2.1 Properties of Equal Proportions

The current method used, the method of equal proportions, was adopted by Congress in 1941 following the 1940 census. This method assigns seats in the House of Representatives per a priority value.

Between 1787 and 1941, five different methods were used to determine the size of each state's delegation to the US of Representatives. In 1941, Congress permanently adopted the Huntington–Hill method, known as the method of equal proportions, which is a mathematical formula to determine apportionment. "The National Academy of Sciences recommended this method." The method of equal proportions was later challenged by the state of Montana; the United States Supreme Court unanimously ruled in 1992 that the method of equal proportions, which shows minimal bias toward small and large states, was constitutional (US Department of Commerce v. Montana, No. 91-860, 1992). The statistical analysis in this book supports the US Supreme Court's decision regarding this method.

///

The method of constructing a priority list to apportion seats using the method of equal proportions involves first computing the reciprocals of the geometric means [$\sqrt{(n(n-1))}$], where n = delegation seats, consisting of consecutive whole numbers used to calculate the geometric mean. For example, $n = 2$;

2.1 Properties of Equal Proportions, *cont.*

$\sqrt{(2(2-1))} = 1.41421346$. The reciprocal of the geometric mean is equal to 0.70710678, which is called the multiplier (see Tables 2.2.1 and 2.2.2). Multipliers are computed for each seat, starting with 51 to 435; each state will receive a delegation of at least one in the House of Representatives, no matter its population. The geometric mean, compared to the arithmetic mean, takes the square root of the count product. The arithmetic mean takes the sum of the values and divides it by the number of items. The geometric mean is between an arithmetic mean and a harmonic mean.[1] It is widely used in science, financial reporting, biology, population growth, and other fields. It characterizes the central tendency theory and provides a dampening effect on very large or low values, such as those seen in the huge population variations among the states. Many mathematicians see the geometric mean as favoring smaller numbers, and, although this may be correct, it gives voice to smaller states and has inconsequential bias against larger states.

///

To construct the "priority list," each state's apportionment population is multiplied by each of the multipliers. The resulting priority values are ranked in descending order (highest to lowest) to show each state's claim to seats in the House. The resulting list expands to the number of available seats, which is 435. The number of seats are reshuffled among states based on their population to fit proportionally within the 435 available seats.

After all priority values have been computed, a list of priority values from every state is ranked in descending order. The state with the largest priority value is given the 51st seat (because the first 50 seats are automatically assigned); then, the state with the second-largest priority value is given the 52nd seat, and so on. This process is continued for each consecutively descending priority value until the last (435th) seat has been filled. The state composition of the reapportioned House of Representatives is then complete.

///

As shown in Figure 2.1.1, the model is simple, yet it is rigorous and powerful. Its use in determining proportionality in the apportionment process for the

[1] Harmonic mean (H) = 2(A*B/A+B).

2.1 Properties of Equal Proportions, *cont.*

US House of Representatives and many financial appropriations to states by Congress is palpable. In addition, the proportionality it brings to the Electoral College not only is a mathematical feat but also is compatible with the United States' republic form of government. The mathematical priority value model was derived from the Huntington–Hill method.

$$\text{Priority value} = [1/\sqrt{n(n-1)}](\text{population})$$

$$\text{where } [1/\sqrt{n(n-1)}] \text{ is the multiplier}$$

$$\therefore \text{Priority value} = (\text{multiplier})(\text{state's population})$$

Figure 2.1.1: Priority Value Model.[1]

In the Electoral College, the number of electors is based primarily on the method of equal proportions, which has been upheld by the US Supreme Court as constitutional; thus, it is an objective and fair method for determining the number of electors from each state. In this book, I used the method of equal proportions to make a compelling and objective case for continuing the Electoral College process to elect the US president and vice president. Furthermore, it provides an excellent ratio scale for each state's popular vote to elect the US president and vice president.

2.2 Determining the Allocation of Electors (Example)

This section utilizes a computational example of the method of equal proportions to determine the allocations of electors per state. The mathematical model shown in Figure 2.1.1 works well for the 50 states or any number of states; therefore, in the interest of time, the example computed in this section assumes a three-state country. The example provides close-up details and the rigor of the method of equal proportions.

///

Example: Assume that there are three states in the Union (Kansas, Wisconsin, and South Carolina) and that the House size is set at 19 representatives. The first seat for each state is assigned by the Constitution; consequently,

[1] See Table 2.2.1, page 8—computation of priority values.

2.2 Determining the Allocation of Electors (Example), *cont.*

the remaining 16 seats must be apportioned using the equal proportions formula. The 2010 US Census apportionment populations for these states were 2,863,813 for Kansas, 5,698,230 for Wisconsin, and 4,645,975 for South Carolina. Table 2.2.1 illustrates how the priority values are computed for each of the three states. Table 2.2.2 illustrates highest priority value is given to the fourth seat (because the first three seats are automatically assigned); then, the state with the second-highest priority value is given the fifth seat, and so on. The resulting ranking is numbered, and seats are assigned until the total of 19 seats is reached (see Tables 2.2.1, 2.2.2, and 2.2.3).

///

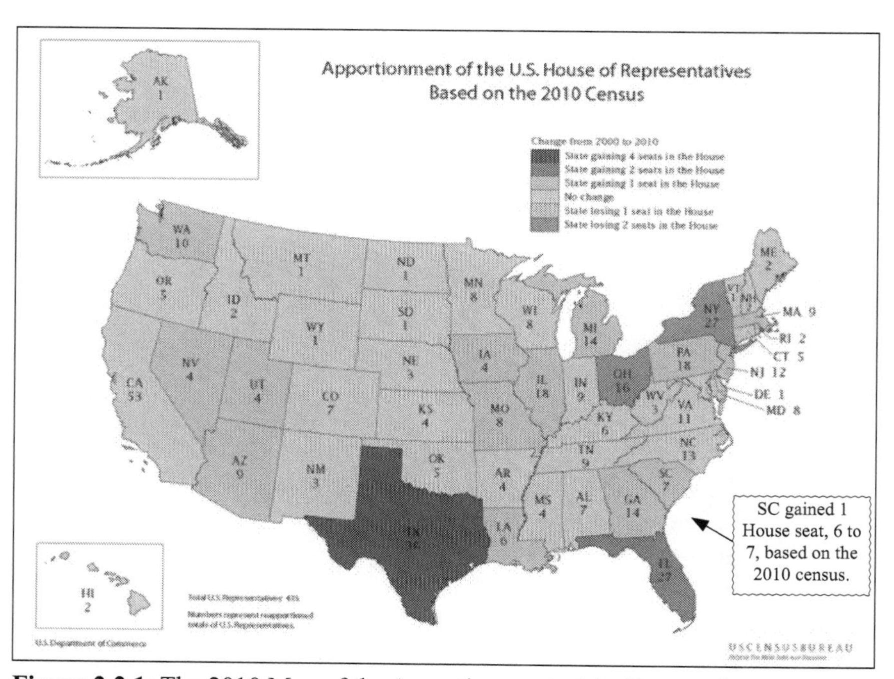

Figure 2.2.1: The 2010 Map of the Apportionment of the House of Representatives.[1]

[1] Source: US Census Bureau, Caroline Population Center.

2.2 Determining the Allocation of Electors (Example), *cont.*

Table 2.2.1: Priority Values Calculations—Calculations of priority values for 19 seats for three states, House delegations using the 2010 census data.

	State's Priority Value Claim to a Delegation Size			
		Calculations		
State	Size Delegation	Multiplier	Population	Priority Value (P·M)[1]
Kansas	2	0.70710678	2,863,813	2,025,022
Kansas	3	0.40824829	2,863,813	1,169,147
Kansas	4	0.28867513	2,863,813	826,712
Kansas	5	0.22360680	2,863,813	640,368
Kansas	6	0.18257419	2,863,813	522,858
Kansas	7	0.15430335	2,863,813	441,896
Kansas	8	0.13363062	2,863,813	382,693
Kansas	9	0.11785113	2,863,813	337,504
Kansas	10	0.10540926	2,863,813	301,872
Kansas	11	0.09534626	2,863,813	273,054
Wisconsin	2	0.70710678	5,698,230	4,029,257
Wisconsin	3	0.40824829	5,698,230	2,326,293
Wisconsin	4	0.28867513	5,698,230	1,644,937
Wisconsin	5	0.22360680	5,698,230	1,274,163
Wisconsin	6	0.18257419	5,698,230	1,040,350
Wisconsin	7	0.15430335	5,698,230	879,256
Wisconsin	8	0.13363062	5,698,230	761,458
Wisconsin	9	0.11785113	5,698,230	671,543
Wisconsin	10	0.10540926	5,698,230	600,646
Wisconsin	11	0.09534626	5,698,230	543,305
Wisconsin	12	0.08703883	5,698,230	495,967
South Carolina	2	0.70710678	4,645,975	3,285,200
South Carolina	3	0.40824829	4,645,975	1,896,711
South Carolina	4	0.28867513	4,645,975	1,341,177
South Carolina	5	0.22360680	4,645,975	1,038,872
South Carolina	6	0.18257419	4,645,975	848,235
South Carolina	7	0.15430335	4,645,975	716,890
South Carolina	8	0.13363062	4,645,975	620,845
South Carolina	9	0.11785113	4,645,975	547,533
South Carolina	10	0.10540926	4,645,975	489,729
South Carolina	11	0.09534626	4,645,975	442,976
South Carolina	13	0.08703883	4,645,975	404,380

[1] Priority values are ranked in descending order in Table 2.2.2. They are calculated by multiplying the state's population by the multiplier [$1/\sqrt{n(n-1)}$], where *n* is the number of seats to be allocated to the state. The multiplier is the reciprocal of the geometric mean.

2.2 Determining the Allocation of Electors (Example), *cont.*

Table 2.2.2: Priority Ranking for Assigning 19 Seats in a Three State House Delegation Scenario (2010 Census). Priority values are arranged in descending order for the 19 seats allocated so that the apportionment can be applied to each of the three states.[1]

	State's Priority Value Claim to a Delegation Size				
			Calculations		
House Seats	State	Size of Delegation	Multiplier	Population	Priority Value (P·M)[2]
4	Wisconsin	2	0.70710678	5,698,230	4,029,257
5	South Carolina	2	0.70710678	4,645,975	3,285,200
6	Wisconsin	3	0.40824829	5,698,230	2,326,293
7	Kansas	2	0.70710678	2,863,813	2,025,022
8	South Carolina	3	0.40824829	4,645,975	1,896,711
9	Wisconsin	4	0.28867513	5,698,230	1,644,937
10	South Carolina	4	0.28867513	4,645,975	1,341,177
11	Wisconsin	5	0.22360680	5,698,230	1,274,163
12	Kansas	3	0.40824829	2,863,813	1,169,147
13	Wisconsin	6	0.18257419	5,698,230	1,040,350
14	South Carolina	5	0.22360680	4,645,975	1,038,872
15	Wisconsin	7	0.15430335	5,698,230	879,256
16	South Carolina	6	0.18257419	4,645,975	848,235
17	Kansas	4	0.28867513	2,863,813	826,712
18	Wisconsin	8	0.13363062	5,698,230	761,458
19	South Carolina	7	0.15430335	4,645,975	716,890

[1] The number of seats shown in the first column of the table has been held to 19. In Table 2.2.1, the number of rows is 32. After the priority values are ranked in descending order in Table 2.2.1, all rows after the 19th are discarded to limit the seats to the required 19, as shown in Table 2.2.2. After these rows are eliminated, the size of each state's delegation is the largest count. For example, Kansas has four seats, Wisconsin has eight seats, and South Carolina has seven seats. The final delegation tally is shown in Table 2.2.3 on page 10. These counts are compared with the previous decennial census for any gains or losses. South Carolina gained one seat because it was at six seats in the 2000 census and in the 2010 census, it had a plus one gain from six to seven seats. The same process is followed for all 50 states to determine the number of seats each state receives.

[2] Priority values are ranked in descending order in Table 2.2.2. They are calculated by multiplying the state's population by the multiplier $[1/\sqrt{n(n-1)}]$, where n is the number of seats to be allocated to the state. The multiplier is the reciprocal of the geometric mean. See Table 2.2.1.

2.2 Determining the Allocations of Electors (Example), *cont.*

Table 2.2.3: Tally of House, Senate, Congress, and Electors for the Three State Example.

House of Representatives	Senators	Total Delegation to Congress	Total Number of Electors
Kansas = 4[1]	Kansas = 2	Kansas = 6	Kansas = 6
Wisconsin = 8[1]	Wisconsin = 2	Wisconsin = 10	Wisconsin = 10
South Carolina = 7[2]	South Carolina = 2	South Carolina = 9	South Carolina = 9

///

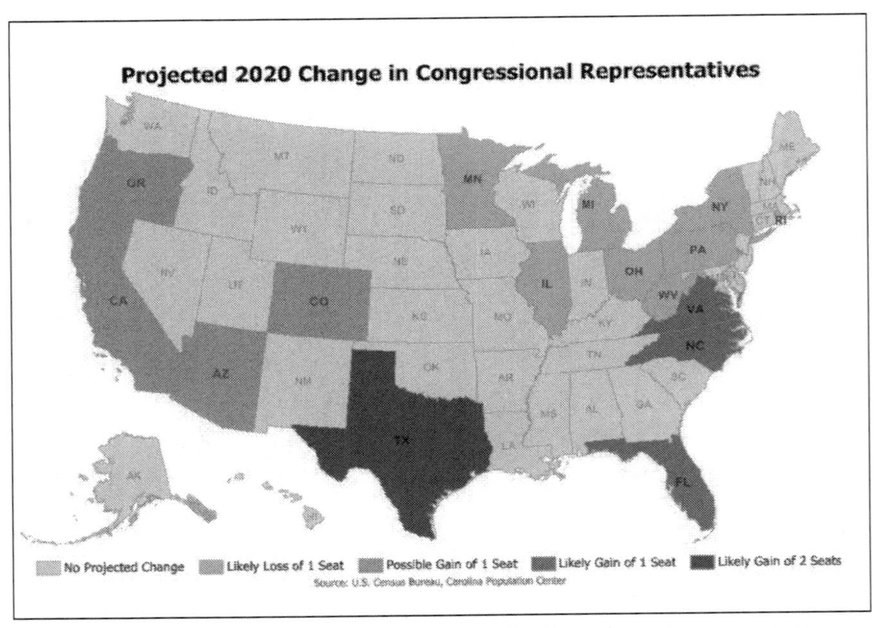

Figure 2.2.2: The 2020 Projected Census Map[3] of the Apportionment of the House of Representatives.[4]

---

[1]In the 2010 census—no change.
[2]In the 2010 census—apportionment changed from six to seven House seats (Figure 2.2.1).
[3]Source: US Census Bureau, Caroline Population Center.
[4]The apportionment population excludes the population of the District of Columbia. The delegation representing the District of Columbia was fixed at three by the 23rd Amendment, which was ratified on March 29, 1961.

Chapter 3

The Power of Electors by State

3.1 Electoral Votes Relative to the Population

The purpose of this chapter is to present readers with sufficient information so they have a clearer understanding of proportionality, voting power, and the role of the Electoral College in electing the US president and vice president. *In this book, voting power is defined as the probability that a single vote is decisive in a winning coalition.* For example, the state of California (55 electoral votes) has the largest population (37,341,989), and Wyoming (three electoral votes) has the smallest population (568,300). Hence, the average number of residents per electoral vote in California is 678,945 and, in Wyoming, 189,433. The population of California is about 66 times larger than the population of Wyoming. As such, the California voter is not 66 times as powerful as the Wyoming voter; rather it is the square root of 66, which equates to 8.11 times as influential as a Wyoming voter. However, California has about 18.33 times more electoral votes than Wyoming, which means that a voter in California is the square root of 18.33, which equates to 4.28 times as influential as a Wyoming voter. What do the 8.11 and 4.28 mean in a two-stage voting process? The Electoral College encompasses such a process, as indicated by California's 8.11 and 4.28 advantages in the popular vote and electoral vote, respectively. Therefore, the two stages are mathematically combined to determine the voting power of each state. Additionally, the ratio of a state's voting power to that of another state's voting power is achieved by dividing the larger state's voting power by the

3.1 Electoral Votes Relative to the Population, *cont.*

smaller state's voting power. Examples are demonstrated in the remainder of this section for the two-stage voting process.

///

Statistical theory says that an individual's voting power, or the probability or likelihood of being a critical voter in a winning coalition within a state is roughly proportional to the multiplicative inverse square root (1/√n), where *n* is the population of the state.

///

Likewise, the Banzhaf power index (BPI[1]) is defined by the probability of changing an outcome of a vote where voting rights are not necessarily equally divided among the voters or shareholders. The BPI fits well in the two-step-voting process (Electoral College) discussed in this book. The BPI model states that an individual voter's probability of being in a state with population *n* is roughly proportional to 1/√n times the BPI of the state. Furthermore, the BPI can be seen as a mathematical representation of how likely it is that a single vote would be able to swing the vote to a winning coalition. Suppose the voting power of a Wyoming voter casting a decisive vote is p; therefore, the process to compute the voting power or probability of an individual voter per state is as follows: An individual voter probability is computed when (1/√n) is multiplied by (a state's BPI). For example, California's BPI is 11.41, and Wyoming's BPI is 0.55. Therefore, the voting power of the individual voter is [(1/√(37,341,989))]*11.41= 0.001867 for California and [(1/√(568,300))]*0.55 = 0.000724 for Wyoming. Computing the voting power ratio between the two states is performed by dividing California's individual voting power by Wyoming's individual voting power (0.001867/0.000724) = 2.58 = 2.58p. This means that the probability of a California voter casting a decisive vote is 2.58 times that of a Wyoming voter casting a decisive vote in a winning coalition for president and vice president.

---

[1] The BPI, named after John F. Banzhaf III [*originally invented by Lionel Penrose in 1946 and sometimes called the Penrose-Banzhaf Index; it is also known as the Banzhaf–Coleman Index after James Samuel Coleman*] is a power index defined by the probability of changing an outcome of a vote where voting rights are necessarily equally divided among the voters or shareholders.

3.1 Electoral Votes Relative to the Population, *cont.*

The example in this paragraph illustrates that the voting power or probability of casting a decisive vote uses a slightly different formula; nevertheless, the results are the same as in the previous paragraph. For example, suppose the voting power of the Wyoming voter of casting a decisive vote is probability *p*; then the California voting power of an individual being decisive in the two-step process is about 21p/8.11= 2.58*p*.[1] Hence, the Wyoming voter's probability is the same answer as in the previous example. The voting power ratio is about three-to-one (3:1). Proof of the ratio is as follows: California's probability is 2.58*p*, which is 2.58 times the Wyoming probability, equaling to 2.58*(0.000724) = 0.001867, which is California's voting power per voter. See Table 3.5.1 (page 22) for the voting power in all 50 states and the District of Columbia.

What about the voting power ratio of New York and South Carolina? Suppose the South Carolina voter's probability of casting a decisive vote is p; then the New York voter's probability of casting the decisive vote is about 3.53*p*/2.84 = 1.24*p*. This means that the New York voting power per voter is 1.24 times South Carolina's probability. Moreover, this process can be used to compare any state with another in finding the ratio of individual voting power between two states. See Table 3.5.1.

This paragraph involves computing the weight[2] of a vote for the 50 states and the District of Columbia. The weight is computed by dividing a state's individual voter's weight by the national voter's weight. A state's individual vote weight is computed by dividing the electoral vote by the population count. The national average vote weight is computed by dividing the total of electoral votes (538) by the national population. Hence, [(EVs/Ps)]/[(EVn/Pn)], which computes to voter weights of 0.85 and 3.04 for California and Wyoming, respectively (Table 3.5.1). The weight of a random voter in California is 0.85, whereas the weight of a random voter in Wyoming

[1] The 2.58*p* was calculated by dividing the BPI ratio of California–Wyoming by the square root of the two populations, ratio. Formula: [(11.41/0.55)]/[√(37,341,989/568,300)] = 21*p*/8.11 = 2.58*p*.
[2] The weight of one vote is computed by dividing the total number of electoral votes by the national population, which equates to 538/309,785,186 = 0.000001736 of a vote. The state's weight is computed by dividing the state's electoral votes by the state's population. For example, the Wyoming weight of one vote is three electors divided by its population of 568,300, which is equal to 0.000005279. Hence, dividing Wyoming by the national population, which equates to the weight of a Wyoming vote, is = 0.000005279/0.000001736 = 3.04. EVn = total national electoral vote; EVs = electoral vote; Ps = state population; Pn = national population. *Note: In the interest of the reader who might not have worked with scientific notation recently, its use in this book is avoided wherever possible.*

3.1 Electoral Votes Relative to the Population, *cont.*

is 3.04. This means that individual votes from Wyoming have (3.04/0.85) = 3.6 times more weight influence than those from California. These computations can be used to compare any state with another in finding the ratio of voter weight between two states. Although California's voter weight is significantly less than Wyoming's, nevertheless California has 2.58 times Wyoming's voting *power*. This is consistent with the idea of proportionality and balance provided by the Electoral College process by giving voice to every state regardless of its size, as guaranteed by Article IV, Section 4 of the US Constitution.

It might appear that small states have an advantage because of higher vote *weight*. For example, the vote *weight* of the California voter is significantly less than that of Wyoming; nevertheless, California, which is allocated 55 electoral votes, would be more likely to swing the vote than a state such as Wyoming or Montana, which have three electoral votes each. Although the small state voter has more *weight* (influence) in choosing electors, those electors are less crucial in casting a ballot that determines the winning coalition or outcome of a presidential election. The graph in Figure 3.3.4 depicts small states (reading from left to right) showing a higher voter weight than large states. Conversely, the graph in Figure 3.3.5 (reading from left to right) shows that large states enjoy more voting *power* than small states. Hence, in the smaller populous states, vote weight is higher than that of large states, but larger states enjoy stronger voting power. To simplify the difference between voter power and voter weight, one can think of vote weight as analogous to potential energy and voting power as analogous to kinetic energy. Mathematically speaking, the two basically meet in the middle, resulting in fairness between small and large states in their voting power in electing a president and vice president (see Figure 3.3.6).

Moreover, California has 55 electoral votes and Wyoming has only three electoral votes, meaning that California has more voting power in deciding an election, as would be expected because of its population. Without the Electoral College, smaller states would have virtually no power. It appears that the missing link in the anti-Electoral College debate is that this country was founded as a constitutional republic, not a pure democracy, which was governed by electors who were voted for by the people and for the people based on a proportional representation system that was fair to the population of each state. Article IV, Section 4 of the US Constitution clearly guarantees a republican form of government to each state.

3.2 Effectiveness of the Electoral College

The Electoral College, which may not be perfect, has served the republican form of government in the United States for more than 200 years and has prevented a possible tyrannical government from being formed. It seems that Article II, Section 1, including the 12th Amendment, and Article IV, Section 4 of the US Constitution are complementary to each other, and the elimination of either one could usher in a tyrannical situation. Here is the text of Article IV, Section 4 of the US Constitution: *The United States shall guarantee to every State in this Union a Republican Form of Government, and shall protect each of them against Invasion; and on Application of the Legislature, or of the Executive (when the Legislature cannot be convened), against domestic Violence.*

The graph in Figure 3.3.1 shows a significantly right-skewed population distribution of all 50 states and the District of Columbia. Furthermore, if the House seats and the electors were plotted in a column graph, they would exhibit the same right-skewed distribution shown in Figure 3.3.1. The distribution (see Figure 3.3.4) shows that smaller states have greater vote weight than large states, whereas the graph in Figure 3.3.5 shows that larger states have more voting power than small states. However, the Electoral College's two-step process allows weighted votes to even out the voting power across all the states (see Figure 3.3.6). The weighted vote forces a presidential candidate to recognize small states as well as large states. Therefore, considering the skewness of the distribution shown in Figure 3.3.1, to simply use a majority of a popular vote to elect a president and vice president could potentially incapacitate more than half of the states' ability to have a voice in electing a president and vice president. This means voiding all possibilities of their vote having an impact on a winning coalition.

///

Moreover, Figures 3.3.2 and 3.3.3 show distribution of the population and count for all 50 states and the District of Columbia (DC). The gap in population (Figure 3.3.2) of the largest 12 states and the smallest 38 plus DC shows a much smaller percentage gap between the population is 18 percentage points. The gap in the number of states associated these two populations (Figure 3.3.3) is 42 percentage points. The graphs shown in this chapter illustrate the power of the two-step process in electing a president and vice president of the United States. The graphs highlight the profound unevenness among populations of the 50 states, including the District of Columbia. Furthermore, the graph in Figure 3.3.1, which exhibits a severely non-normal distribution among the population of states, shows that, given the popular vote scenario, about 12 states would potentially

3.2 Effectiveness of the Electoral College, *cont.*

overshadow the other 38 sovereign states which also have a republican form of government. Mathematically, to simply do a tally with a national popular vote to determine the US president and vice president would not make any sense. For example, the last column bar to the right in Figure 3.3.1 represents California with 37 million people, of whom about 14 million voted in the 2016 presidential election. Given today's pattern of voting, about five large states, including California could form a winning coalition that could perpetually tip the popular vote to a majority for one party in every presidential election almost forever. All indications are that the Electoral College provides a damping effect on what would be a lopsided presidential election and serves as a firewall against voter fraud. To emphasize the notion of a popular vote generally does not consider the fact that each state is a sovereign state among a confederation of states, each having its own government and the right to have a voice as specified in the US Constitution.

///

The histogram shown in Figure 3.3.1 depicts the pattern of the populations of states within a specified range of sizes, and the smaller states, as expected, are clustered together to the left of the graph. The graphs in Figure 3.3.2 (population), Figure 3.3.3 (cluster of states), and Figure 3.3.7 (the actual number of votes cast in 2016) demonstrate that about 38 smaller states and the District of Columbia would be overwhelmed by about 12 larger states in electing a president and vice president. In smaller populous states, an individual vote weight is heavier than that in larger states (see Figure 3.3.4). However, Figure 3.3.5 indicates increasing voting power for voters in the more populous states, which means that voting in larger states is not diminished below proportionate bounds.

The graph in 3.3.6 shows all 50 states, including the District of Columbia, arranged from left-to-right with the smaller states starting on the left of the graph. On the right side of the graph are the large states, with California the largest by far with more than 37 million people. Incorporating the BPI to compute the voting power of an individual voter shifts the power of the vote so that every state will have a voice. This is significant because it forces candidates to give voice to every state in their effort to put together a winning coalition provided by the Electoral College. Each state's electoral vote is part of a coalition because each candidate running for president looks across the country to put together a winning coalition; in doing so, he or she gives voice to every state. This kind of voice, which reaches all states, can only be achieved through the Electoral College process where each state has the opportunity of being part of a winning coalition.

3.3 Graphical Analysis of Voting Power

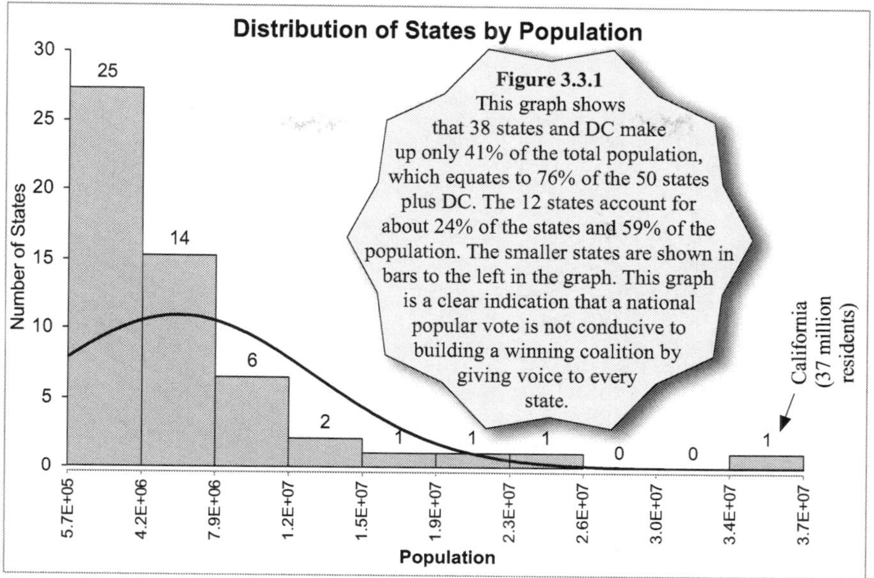

Figure 3.3.1: Distribution of the Percentage of Electors by State. The histogram depicts the total number of states within specified ranges, and the smaller states (left two bars) comprise 38 states and the District of Columbia (DC), with populations having fewer than 8 million residents per state.

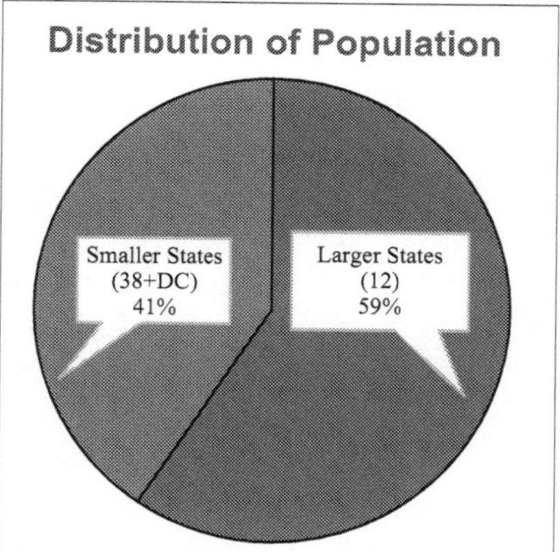

Figure 3.3.2: Population of Larger and Smaller States. A visual view of the larger states should the election be determined by popular vote. The gap is 18 percentage points. US Census 2010, Population 309,885,186. Only 42% of votes cast in the 2016 US presidentail election were from the 38 smmalest states and DC. and an astonding 58% were cast by 12 states.

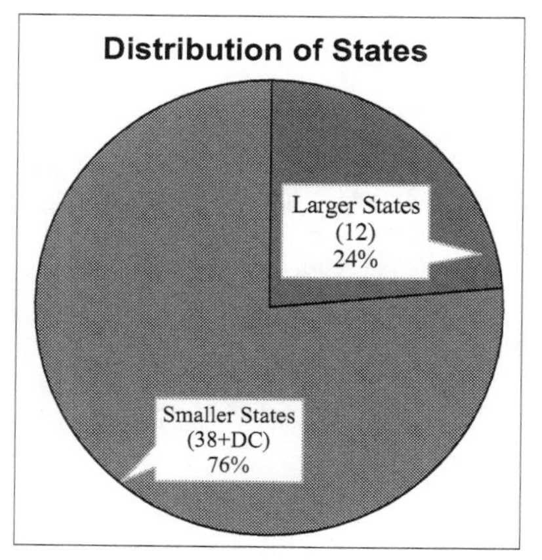

Figure 3.3.3: The Number and Percentage Distribution of Larger and Smaller States. The larger states have a smaller count but 59% of the population, wheras the smaller state count is more three times that of lager states but comprise of only 41% of the population and 42% of total votes cast in 2016 (see Figure 3.3.7, page 20).

3.3 Graphical Analysis of Voting Power, *cont.*

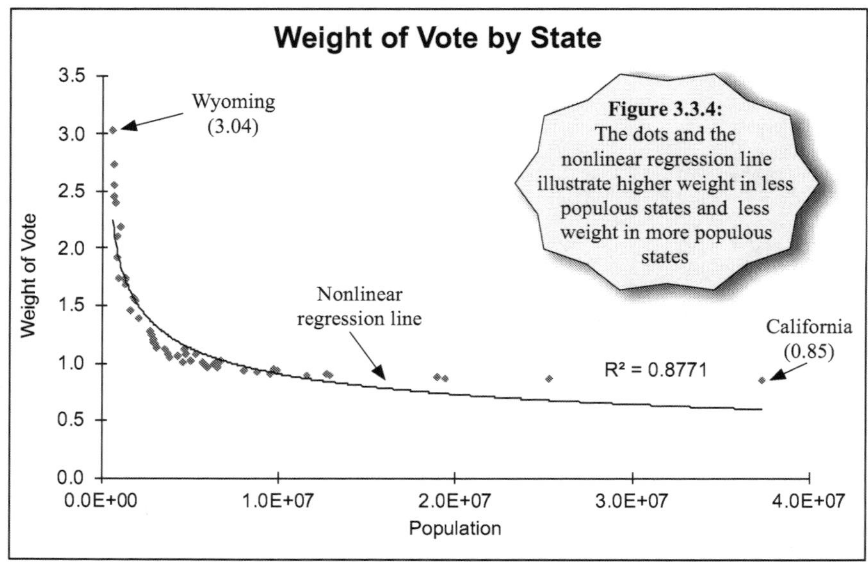

Figure 3.3.4: Nonlinear Regression Analysis[1] of the Weight of a Vote Relative to the Population per State. R-squared value = 0.8771 or 87.7%

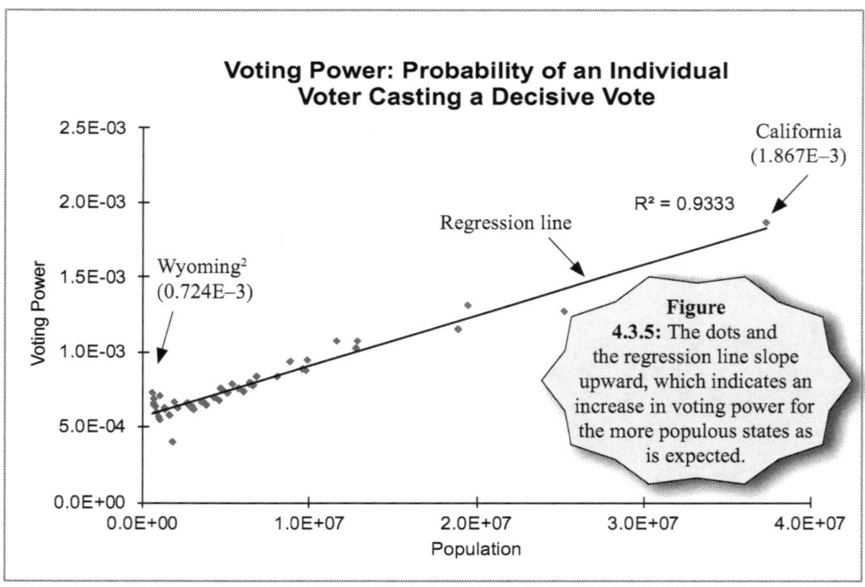

Figure 3.3.5: Linear Regression Analysis[1] Relative to Probability of Voter Casting a Decisive Vote per State. The graph shows an increasing voting power from the less to the more populous states, as expected. The R-squared value = 0.9333, or 93.3% and a $p < 0.0001$.

[1]Regression analysis is covered in Chapter 4.

[2]Wyoming is in located in this cluster of dots.

3.3 Graphical Analysis of Voting Power, *cont*

For example (Figure 3.3.6), if a popular vote were used then the 40 states to the left would have very little voice in electing a president and vice president because it would be impossible for a presidential candidate to build a winning coalition. Hence, the voting power (dotted line) indicates (Figure 3.3.6) that all states receive their voting power through the Electoral College process, whereas the population line (popular vote) proves that some states will have no voice in the process. The graph in Figure 3.3.6 depicts the equalizing effect of voting power in the two-step process, which neutralizes the notion of a popular vote. This is mathematical proof that simply going to a popular vote would not only take away the voice of the people but would also contradict Article IV, Section 4 of the US Constitution, which guarantees a republican form of government to every state in the union. In addition, the Electoral College method, which was established under the US Constitution Article II, Section 1, would need to be rescinded. Hence, the founders made it difficult to change the constitution from the current republican form of government.

///

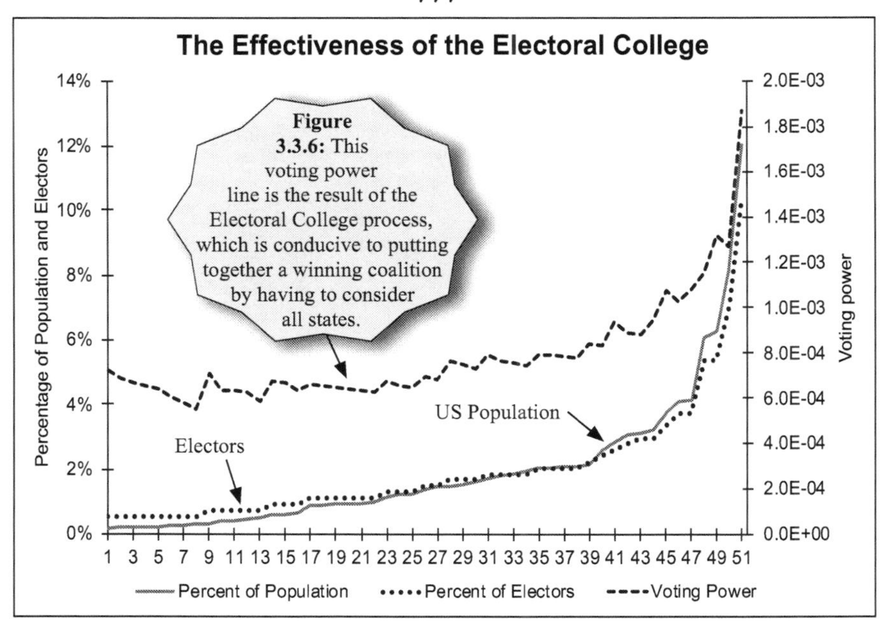

Figure 3.3.6: Popular Vote versus Electoral College Process. The Electoral College weighted-vote methodology evens out the lopsided population distribution shown in Figure 3.3.1 with the Figure in 3.3.6. Hence, Wyoming is indicated by the number one on the far left and California is indicated by the number 51 on the far right (*x*-axis). The voting power line shows proportionate increases in voting power.

3.3 Graphical Analysis of Voting Power, *cont.*

The graph below shows the number of votes cast in the 2016 presidential election. This graph is consistent with the graph in Figure 3.3.1, which depicts the right-skewed population. Considering the current voting pattern, it is possible that California alone could perpetually tip a popular vote for one party (see Figure 3.3.7).

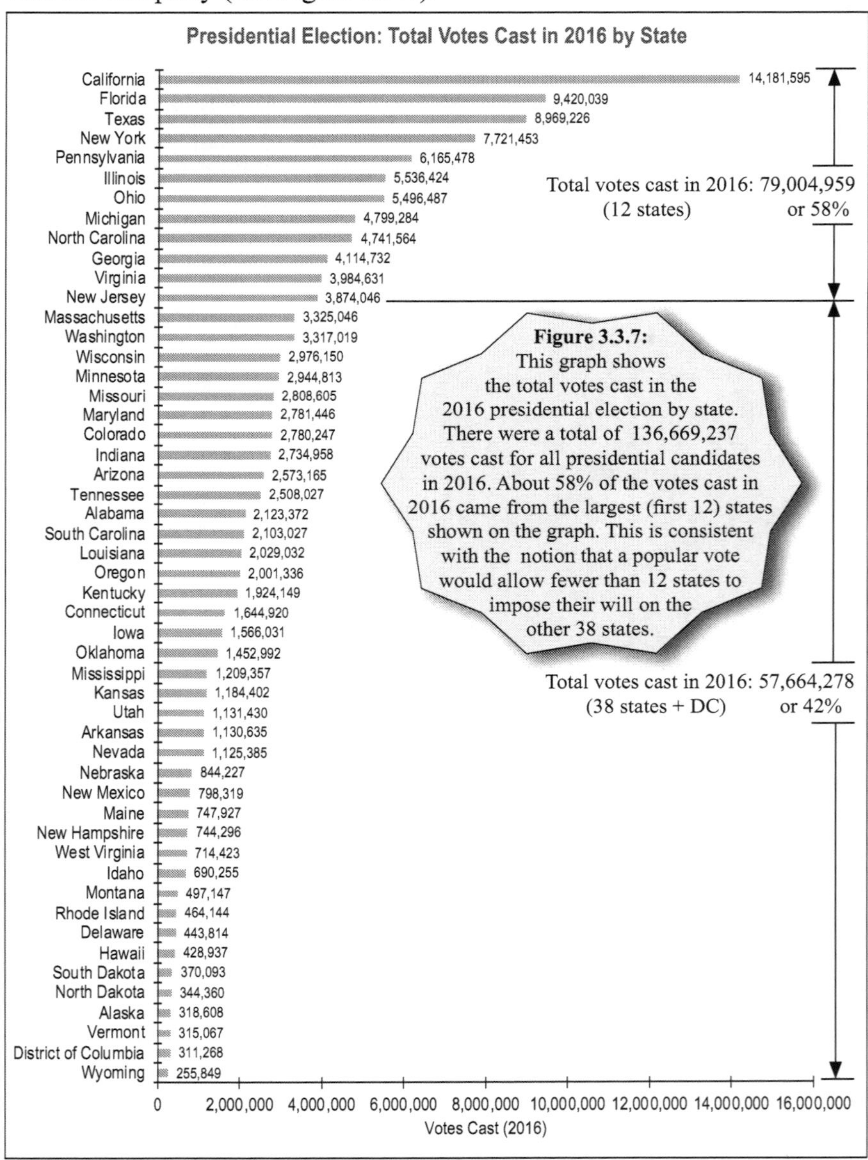

Figure 3.3.7: Popular Vote Cast in 2016 by State. See Figure 4.3.7 (page 32) for percentage distribution of votes cast versus the population.

3.4 Electoral College and a Winning Coalition

Merriam-Webster's dictionary defines "coalition" as a temporary alliance of distinct parties, persons, or states for joint action. In this book, coalition means any slate of electoral votes combined from the various states to garner the 270 electoral votes required for a person to be elected president and vice president of the United States. A winning coalition in this example is the candidate who earned a minimum of 270 electoral votes, and the losing coalition is the one who garnered fewer than 270 electoral votes.

The example shown below shows why the Electoral College process gives voice to all states because each candidate is forced to put together a winning coalition by listening to the voices of people from all of the states. For example, in the 2002 election there was a five-electoral-vote difference between the winning and losing coalition, which was 271 to 266, with one elector abstaining in the official tally (Bush v. Gore 2000). This example emphasizes the importance of Article II, Section 1 and Article IV, Section 4 of the US Constitution. These articles established the Electoral College and guaranteed every state a republican form of government, respectively. However, a popular vote method would contradict Articles II and IV. Mathematically speaking, the total number of votes cast in a presidential election is inconsequential in electing a president and vice president. The disparity in size of these sovereign states, as shown in Figures 3.3.1, 3.3.2, 3.3.3, and 3.3.7 amplifies the notion that the total number of people who voted for one candidate or the other is unimportant. Considering the level of disparity shown in these figures, a popular vote will most likely be fraught with voter fraud.

Let S represent a state's electors who are in the X or Y coalition. This means that a candidate will cover the entire nation with visits, surrogates, robocalls, campaign ads, and so on to small and large states in an effort to put together a winning coalition of 270 electoral votes. Hence, every state's voice is heard (Figure 3.3.6). The following calculations illustrate the lesson learned about electoral votes (Bush v. Gore in 2000):

Electoral College $\{S_1, S_2, S_3, \ldots S_n\}$

<u>Winning Coalition</u>

- Presidential Candidate X: [270; 38, 29, 12, . . . 3]
  $S_1 + S_2 + S_3 + \ldots + S_n = 38 + 29 + 20 + \ldots + 3 = 306 \geq 270$

<u>Losing Coalition</u>

- Presidential Candidate Y: [270; 38, 29, 12, . . . 3]
  $S_4 + S_5 + S_6 + \ldots + S_n = 55 + 29 + 14 + \ldots + 3 = 232 < 270$

3.5 Tabular Analysis of Electors by State

Table 3.5.1: Comparative Analyses of Electors by State. Residents per elector, comparison of California's population, electors, percentage of electors, weight of voter, BPI, and voting power.

State	Population[1]	Electors	Percentage of Electors	California Pop Voter Influence[2]	California EC Voter Influence[2]	California's BPI Ratio to States[3]	Banzhaf Power Index[4]	Weight of Vote[5]	California's Voting Power Ratio[6]	Voting Power[7]
Alabama	4,802,982	9	1.67	2.79	2.47	7p	1.64	1.08	2.50p	0.000748
Alaska	721,523	3	0.56	7.19	4.28	21p	0.55	2.39	2.90p	0.000643
Arizona	6,412,700	11	2.04	2.41	2.24	6p	2.00	0.99	2.36p	0.000790
Arkansas	2,926,229	6	1.12	3.57	3.03	10p	1.09	1.18	2.93p	0.000637
California†	37,341,989	55	10.22	1.00	1.00	1p	11.41	0.85	1.00p	0.001867
Colorado	5,044,930	9	1.67	2.72	2.47	7p	1.64	1.03	2.56p	0.000730
Connecticut	3,581,628	7	1.30	3.23	2.80	9p	1.27	1.13	2.77p	0.000673
Delaware	900,877	3	0.56	6.44	4.28	21p	0.55	1.92	3.25p	0.000575
District of Columbia	601,723	3	0.56	7.29	4.28	21p	0.55	2.87	2.86p	0.000652
Florida	18,900,773	29	5.39	1.41	1.38	2p	5.02	0.88	1.62p	0.001154
Georgia	9,727,566	16	2.97	1.96	1.85	4p	2.74	0.95	2.13p	0.000879
Hawaii	1,366,862	4	0.74	5.23	3.71	16p	0.73	1.69	2.99p	0.000624
Idaho	1,573,499	4	0.74	4.87	3.71	16p	0.73	1.46	3.21p	0.000582
Illinois	12,864,380	20	3.72	1.70	1.66	3p	3.87	0.90	1.73p	0.001079
Indiana	6,501,582	11	2.04	2.40	2.24	6p	2.00	0.97	2.38p	0.000784
Iowa	3,053,787	6	1.12	3.50	3.03	10p	1.09	1.13	2.99p	0.000624
Kansas	2,863,813	6	1.12	3.61	3.03	10p	1.09	1.21	2.90p	0.000644
Kentucky	4,350,606	8	1.49	2.93	2.62	8p	1.46	1.06	2.67p	0.000699
Louisiana	4,553,962	8	1.49	2.86	2.62	8p	1.46	1.01	2.73p	0.000683
Maine	1,333,074	4	0.74	5.29	3.71	16p	0.73	1.73	2.96p	0.000631
Maryland	5,789,929	10	1.86	2.54	2.35	6p	1.82	0.99	2.46p	0.000758
Massachusetts	6,559,644	11	2.04	2.39	2.24	6p	2.00	0.97	2.39p	0.000781
Michigan	9,911,626	16	2.97	1.94	1.85	4p	2.97	0.93	1.98p	0.000945
Minnesota	5,314,879	10	1.86	2.65	2.35	6p	1.82	1.08	2.36p	0.000791
Mississippi	2,978,240	6	1.12	3.54	3.03	10p	1.09	1.16	2.96p	0.000632
Missouri	6,011,478	10	1.86	2.49	2.35	6p	1.82	0.96	2.51p	0.000744

Table 3.5.1—cont. on next page

1, 2, 3, 4, 5, 6, 7: See footnotes on page 24.

3.5 Tabular Analysis of Electors by State, *cont.*

Table 3.5.1: (cont.)

State	Population[1]	Electors	Percentage of Electors	California Pop Voter Influence[2]	California EC Voter Influence[2]	California's BPI Ratio to States[3]	Banzhaf Power Index[4]	Weight of Vote[5]	California's Voting Power Ratio[6]	Voting Power[7]
Montana	994,416	3	0.56	6.13	4.28	21p	0.55	1.74	3.41p	0.000548
Nebraska	1,831,825	5	0.53	4.51	3.32	21p	0.55	1.57	4.63p	0.000403
Nevada	2,709,432	6	1.12	3.71	3.03	10p	1.09	1.28	2.81p	0.000663
New Hampshire	1,321,445	4	0.74	5.32	3.71	16p	0.73	1.74	2.95p	0.000633
New Jersey	8,807,501	14	2.60	2.06	1.98	4p	2.79	0.92	1.99p	0.000939
New Mexico	2,067,273	5	0.93	4.25	3.32	13p	0.91	1.39	2.95p	0.000633
New York	19,421,055	29	5.39	1.39	1.38	2p	5.79	0.86	1.42p	0.001315
North Carolina	9,565,781	15	2.79	1.98	1.91	4p	2.74	0.90	2.10p	0.000887
North Dakota	675,905	3	0.56	7.43	4.28	21p	0.55	2.56	2.81p	0.000664
Ohio	11,568,495	18	3.35	1.80	1.75	3p	3.67	0.90	1.73p	0.001078
Oklahoma	3,764,882	7	1.30	3.15	2.80	9p	1.27	1.07	2.84p	0.000657
Oregon	3,848,606	7	1.30	3.11	2.80	9p	1.27	1.05	2.88p	0.000649
Pennsylvania	12,734,905	20	3.72	1.71	1.66	3p	3.68	0.90	1.81p	0.001030
Rhode Island	1,055,247	4	0.74	5.95	3.71	16p	0.73	2.18	2.63p	0.000709
South Carolina	4,645,975	9	1.67	2.84	2.47	7p	1.64	1.12	2.45p	0.000761
South Dakota	819,761	3	0.56	6.75	4.28	21p	0.55	2.11	3.10p	0.000603
Tennessee	6,375,431	11	2.04	2.42	2.24	6p	2.01	0.99	2.35p	0.000794
Texas	25,268,418	38	7.06	1.22	1.20	2p	6.39	0.87	1.47p	0.001272
Utah	2,770,765	6	1.12	3.67	3.03	10p	1.09	1.25	2.85p	0.000656
Vermont	630,337	3	0.56	7.70	4.28	21p	0.55	2.74	2.72p	0.000688
Virginia	8,037,736	13	2.42	2.16	2.06	5p	2.37	0.93	2.23p	0.000836
Washington	6,753,369	12	2.23	2.35	2.14	5p	2.19	1.02	2.22p	0.000843
West Virginia	1,859,815	5	0.93	4.48	3.32	13p	0.91	1.55	2.80p	0.000667

Table 3.5.1—cont. on next page

1, 2, 3, 4, 5, 6, 7: See footnotes on page 24.

3.5 Tabular Analysis of Electors by State, *cont.*

Table 3.5.1: (cont.)

State	Population[1]	Electors	Percentage of Electors	California Pop Voter Influence[2]	California EC Voter Influence[2]	California's BPI Ratio to States[3]	Banzhaf Power Index[4]	Weight of Vote[5]	California's Voting Power Ratio[6]	Voting Power[7]
Wisconsin	5,698,230	10	1.86	2.56	2.35	6p	1.82	1.01	2.44p	0.000764
Wyoming	568,300	3	0.56	8.11	4.28	21p	0.55	3.04	2.58p	0.000724
Total	309,785,186	538	100%				100	100		

[1] United States 2010 census resident population, including the District of Columbia, is 309,785,186.

[2] A voter in California is more influential times the corresponding listed state in the first column. Pop = population and EC = Electoral College

[3] California's BPI ratio to other states.

[4] BPI for each state and District of Columbia. The percentage of Electoral College votes mirrors closely the BPI, which is in percentage. The BPI mathematical method supports the Electoral College process. Any mathematical detail about this index is beyond the scope of this book.

[5] The weight of a vote is computed by dividing the national average weight of a vote, which equates to 538/309,785,186 = 0.000001736 of an elector. For example, Wisconsin's weight of one vote is 10 electors divided by its population of 5,698,230, which is equal to 0.000001755. Therefore, the weight of a Wisconsin vote is 0.000001736 divided by 0.000001755 = 1.01. This means that a Wisconsin voter (1.01) has more influence than a California voter (0.85) in casting a ballot that determines a winning coalition.

[6] California's voting power ratio to other states. This means that California's voting power probability is the indicated magnitude times that of other states.

[7] Voting power is the probability of one vote changing the outcome of an election in a block voting situation such as the Electoral College.

Chapter 4

Evidence of Proportionality

4.1 Description

The Electoral College's proportionality of electors depends primarily on the quality of the apportionment process in assigning seat counts for each state. The information presented in this chapter, including the graphs, is evidence that each state is well represented proportionally by the current system for electing the US president and vice president. The analytical and graphical evidence presented in this chapter show that the method of equal proportions is unbiased and represents a sound proportional representation for each state, including the power of the voter as discussed in Chapter 3 of this book. The analysis in this book supports the conclusion of the courts, John F. Banzhaf III, and many mathematicians with expertise in this method.

To show evidence of proportionality, a simple linear regression analysis[1] and chi-square goodness-of-fit test was performed to determine whether

[1] Regression analysis is a statistical process for estimating the relationships among variables. It is a statistical measure of how close data are to the fitted regression line. In linear regression, the data need not be normally distributed—only the residuals of the y-variable need to be normally distributed. To comply with testing for proportionality, the y-intercept of the regression line was forced to zero (0,0). The variables in this analysis are the population, House apportionment, and electors. Additionally, nonparametric regression analysis was used to test for proportionality (equality of slopes) because of its compatibility with non-normal data. Consequently, there were no discernible differences between the parametric linear regression and the nonparametric linear regression; therefore, I published the linear regression analysis and chi-square test results to prove proportionality and voting power. Any tutorial on regression analysis and chi-square testing is beyond the scope of this book. The graphs provide visuals to the reader for evidence of proportionality between the population (popular vote) and the Electoral College (electoral vote).

4.1 Description, *cont.*

the Electoral College process is equivalent to the popular vote method. In regression analysis testing, the strength between two variables is investigated. The coefficient of determination known as R-squared (R^2), which measures the strength in percentage between the variables, is a statistical measure of how close the data are to the fitted regression line. If $R^2 = 0$, it suggests there is no relationship between the Electoral College process and the popular vote method. If $R^2 \neq 0$, it suggests there is a relationship between the Electoral College process and the popular vote method. A regression analysis evaluates the R-squared value to determine its statistical significance. The graphs and their accompanying description depict the following: (1) a positive sloped line, (2) $R^2 \neq 0$ (strength of relationship), and (3) the p-value (p). The parameters that helped determine the significance of the results in proving proportionality are the following: (1) graph: straight line sloping upward; (2) R-squared: $0 \leq R^2 \leq 1$; and (3) p-value: $0 \leq p \leq 1$. A small $p < 0.05$) indicates strong evidence against the null hypothesis of no slope; therefore, one would reject the null hypothesis of no proportionality between the Electoral College process and the popular vote method.

///

As a second test, a chi-square goodness-of-fit test was performed to compare its results from those obtained from regression analysis testing. The chi-square goodness-of-fit test was performed to determine homogeneity between the three parameters, which means the null hypothesis assumes no significant difference exists in the proportionality of the population, House seats, and electors. Therefore, the chi-square test showed no differences between the proportions of these entities ($p = 0.999 > 0.05$); therefore, proof of proportionality mirrors that of the regression analysis testing results shown in the graphs depicted in Figures 4.3.2–4.3.6.

///

As will be shown in this chapter, there is a strong proportional relationship between the Electoral College (electoral vote) and the population (popular vote). The testing results provide strong mathematical evidence that the Electoral College process is an appropriate representation of the voters from each state. This means that the Electoral College process has a huge upside by giving voice to states with smaller populations (Figure 3.3.6, page 19), whereas a popular vote would not give voice to those states. This means that each state, under the US Constitution (Article IV, Section 4),

4.1 Description, *cont.*

has power over itself, and its state government is under its own control, rather than under the control of an outside authority. Constitutionally, each state should continue to have the right to send a slate of electors, based on the size of its population, to vote for the US president and vice president.

All graphs in this chapter were generated directly or indirectly from the data in Table 3.5.1, page 22. The analyses provide visual and statistical evidence of proportionality relative to the population of each state and its apportionment to the House of Representatives and the electors. The mean (average) of the population (6,076,180) is higher than the population median (4,796,553), which means that the population is right skewed by the larger states (Figure 3.3.1). California, for example, is about eight times larger than the median, with 12% of the US population (2010 Census). The magnitude of the skewness alone makes electing a president by popular vote unwise, and it could severely incapacitate the ability of smaller states to have a voice in electing the US president and vice president. The piechart (Figure 3.3.2) illustrates, mathematically, that about 59% of the population resides in the 12 largest states. Additionally, the bar chart (Figure 3.3.7) demonstrates, mathematically, that about 58% of votes cast for the US president and vice president in 2016 were from the 12 largest states. Therefore, a popular vote would diminish the voice of 38 states (41% of the population). This would allow these 12 states (24%) among the 50, which all have large urban populations, to impose their will on the entire country. To emphasize again, the graphs cited above depict the clear disadvantage smaller states would suffer should the election of the US president and vice president be determined by a nationwide popular vote. Furthermore, the graph in Figure 3.3.6 (page 19) illustrates the difference between a popular vote versus the electoral vote, which gives smaller states a voice while larger states also maintain their power in proportion to their population without infringing upon smaller states.

4.2 Population and Electors

The graph in Figure 3.3.1 shows a profound difference in the population; therefore, a popular vote would clearly tip voting power to large states in electing a president and vice president. The two-step Electoral College process blunts this damage and most likely creates a firewall against the possibility of fraud by taking away the ability for one or two states to find enough popular votes to tip the election. The graph in Figure 3.3.6 illustrates the voting power voters have when casting their vote. On the basis of the analysis in this book, a popular vote would certainly diminish the power

4.2 Population and Electors, *cont.*

of smaller states whereas the Electoral College process gives voice to all states, with the larger states having more power, as expected (Figure 3.3.6, page 19). Given the current division within the country between the political parties, a few large states could keep the same party in power indefinitely. This could enable a few large states to impose their values and will on every other state, severely damaging the idea of a constitutional republic[1] form of government and transforming the United States into a pure democracy.[3]

The graphs in Figures 4.3.2–4.3.6 were generated using regression analysis. The graphs show a strong proportional relationship (99.5%[3]) among all entities relative to population, apportionment, the electors, and BPI. These graphs are strong indications that the House's delegation and electors are proportional to the population of each state. Figures 4.3.1–4.3.6 exhibit a strong proportional relationship for the following pairs of parameters: (1) House apportionment and the population, (2) the electors and the population, (3) the percentage of electors and the population, (4) the BPI and population, and (5) the BPI and the electors. The average mathematical proportional strength (R^2) is strong at about 99.5%. Moreover, Figures 4.3.1 and 4.3.7 depict the percentage of population and votes cast in 2016, respectively.

4.3 Graphical Analysis[4]

The graph (Figures 4.3.1) depicts the same patterns of behavior for the population, House apportionment, and electors, which indicates proportionality. The dotted line (Figure 4.3.1) is the percentage of electors for each state and the District of Columbia (DC). The graphs indicate strong proportional relationships between the population (popular vote), the Electoral College process, and the votes cast in 2016 (4.3.1–4.3.7). Therefore, collectively, the graphs show substantial evidence of proportionality and fairness in the Electoral College process to elect the US president and vice president.

[1] Merriam-Webster's definition: Republic is a government in which supreme power resides in a body of citizens entitled to vote and is exercised by elected officers and representatives responsible to them and governing according to law.

[2] Merriam-Webster's definition: Pure democracy is a government in which the supreme power is vested in the people and exercised by them directly rather than through representatives.

[3] This is a statistical measure (R-squared), which is expressed in percentage and represents the proportion of the variance for a dependent variable that is explained by an independent variable. Hence, it is a measure of how close data are to the fitted regression line.

[4] The graphs shown in this section are not necessarily stretched proportionally, either in the vertical or horizonal vertices.

4.3 Graphical Analysis, *cont.*

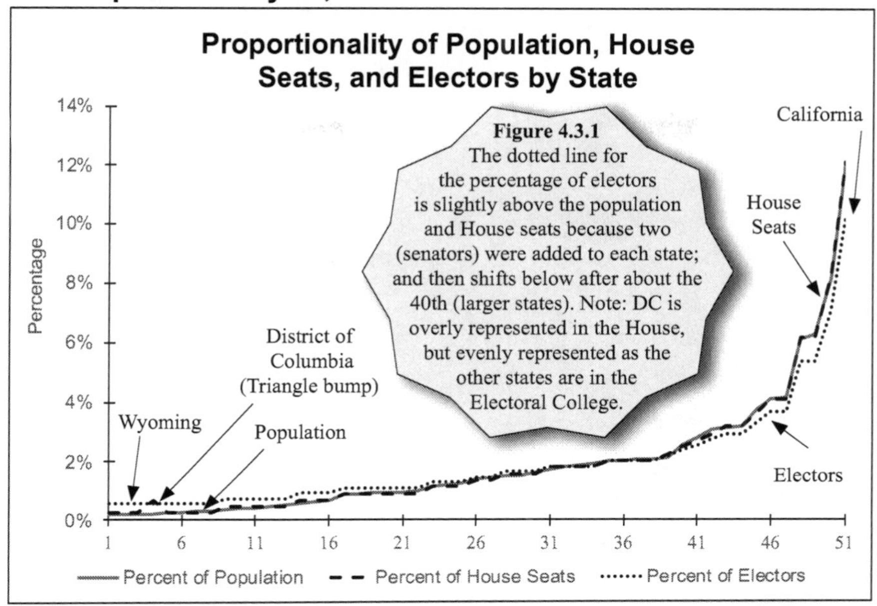

Figure 4.3.1: Proportionality of States' Population, House Seats, and Electors. There is no significant difference between the three entities.

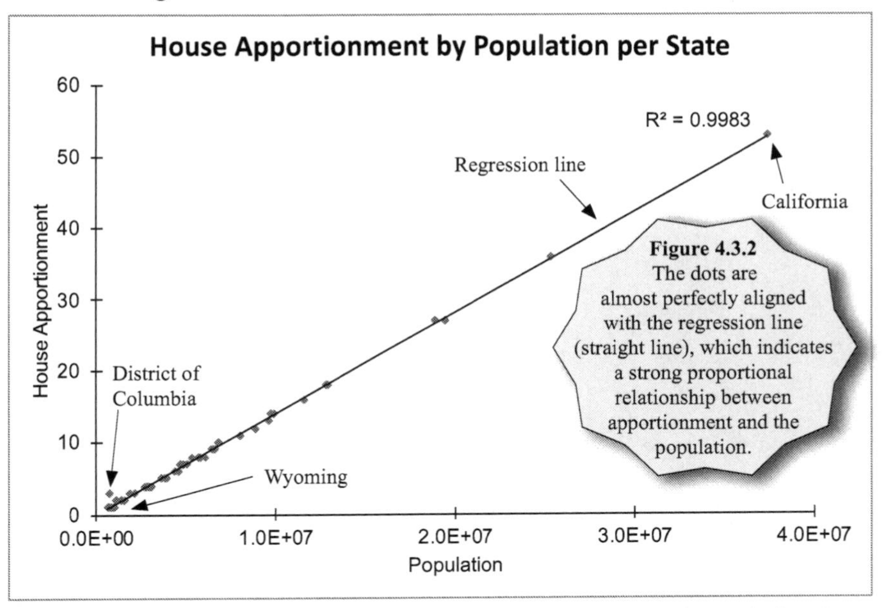

Figure 4.3.2: Regression Analysis Between Apportionment and Population. The regression line plot shows a very strong proportional relationship between the population and apportionment. The R-squared value = 0.9983, or 99.8%, and the reliability of this percentage is validated with hypothesis testing ($p < 0.0001$); therefore, proportionality is strong.

4.3 Graphical Analysis, *cont.*

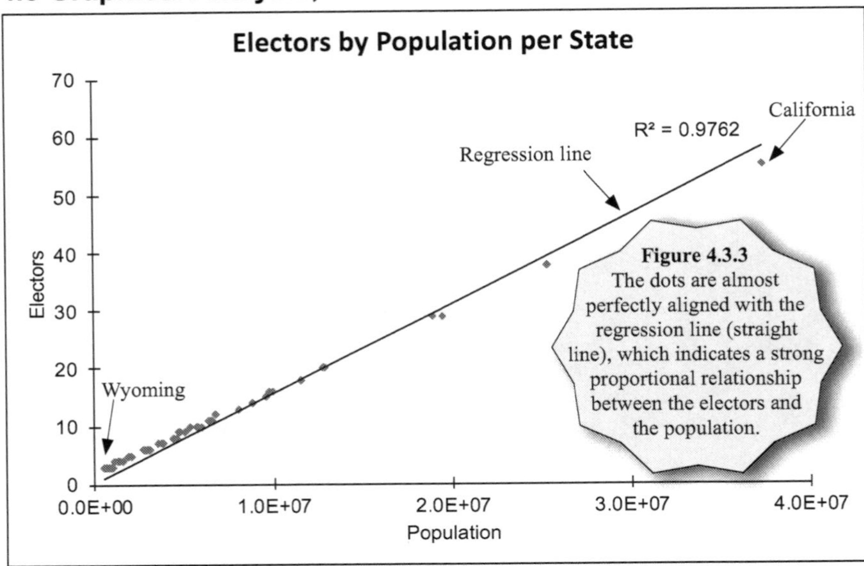

Figure 4.3.3: Regression Analysis Between Electors and Population by State. The regression line shows a strong proportional relationship between the population and the electors with an R-squared value = 0.9762, or 97.6%, and the reliability of this percentage is validated with hypothesis testing ($p < 0.0001$); therefore, proportionality is strong.

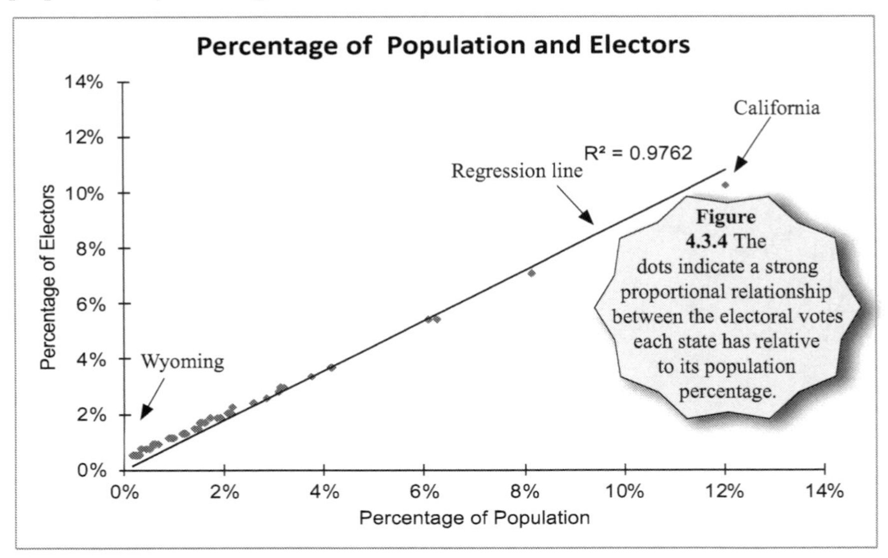

Figure 4.3.4: Regression Analysis Between the Percentage of Electors and Population by State. The regression line shows a very strong proportional relationship between the population and percentage of electors with an R-squared value = 0.9762, or 97.6%, and the reliability of this percentage is validated with hypothesis testing ($p < 0.0001$). Hence, the Electoral College gives voice to every state versus a popular vote whereby every state would not have a voice.

4.3 Graphical Analysis, *cont.*

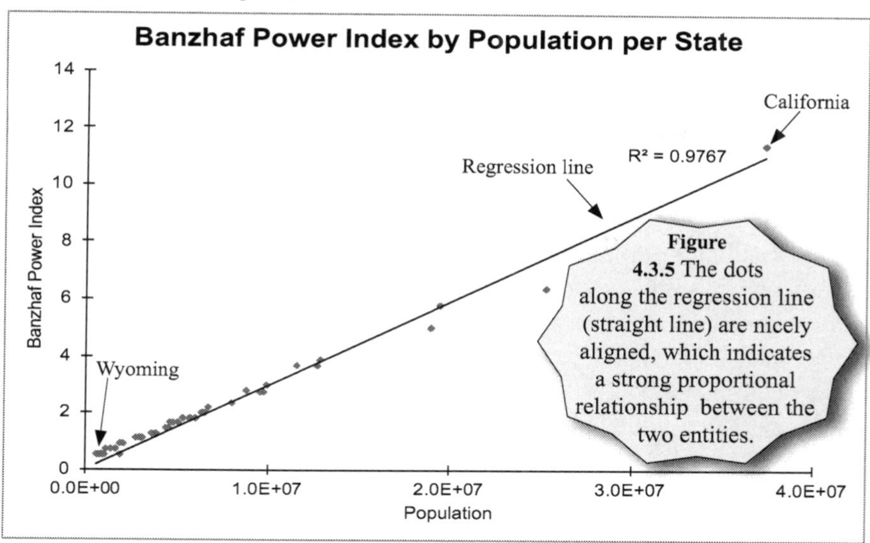

Figure 4.3.5: Regression Analysis Between BPI and Population per State. The regression line shows a strong proportional relationship between the population and the BPI. The R-squared value = 0.9767, or 97.8%, and the reliability of this percentage is validated with hypothesis testing ($p < 0.0001$); therefore, the proportionality relationship is strong.

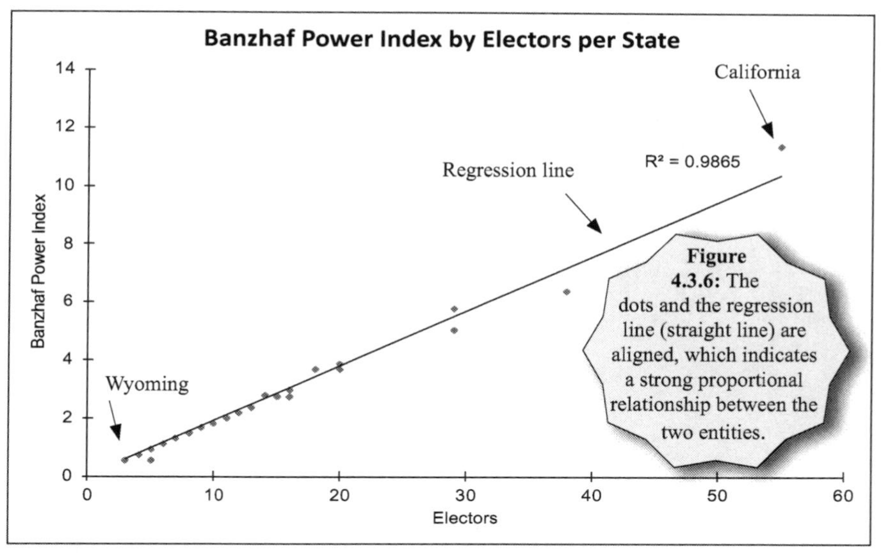

Figure 4.3.6: Regression Analysis Between BPI and Electors per State. The regression line shows a strong proportional relationship between the electors and BPI with an R-squared value = 0.9865, or 98.7%, and the reliability of this percentage is validated with hypothesis testing ($p < 0.0001$); therefore, the proportionality relationship is strong. California is clearly an outlier.

4.3 Graphical Analysis, *cont.*

The graph (Figure 4.3.7) demonstrates an interesting pattern because the percentage of votes cast by each state and DC shows the same pattern as that of the population. Statistically, there is no difference in the number of votes cast per state and the population per state relative to the total votes cast and the total population. This is further evidence that the Electoral College gives voice to every state, versus a national popular vote, which would deprive candidates of the ability to build winning coalitions. Such coalitions cannot be built with a nationwide vote across 50 sovereign states, each with its own interests. The population percentage in California was slightly higher than the percentage of votes cast in the 2016 presidential election; nevertheless, the difference in votes cast and the population proportion per state is statistically insignificant.

Additionally, a regression analysis test was performed on these data, and it also depicted a strong proportional relationship between the votes cast in 2016 and the population, with an R-squared = 0.9983 or 99.8% and p = 0.0001. The results of this test were almost identical to those shown in Figure 4.3.6.

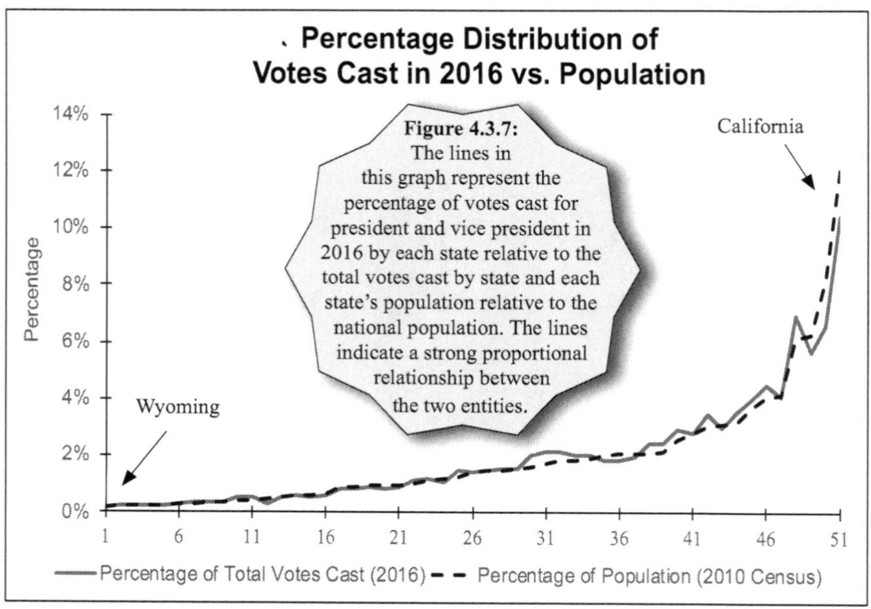

Figure 4.3.7: Percentage Distribution of Votes Cast in 2016 vs. Population per State. The percentage is relative to total votes cast and total population. Smaller to larger states read from left to right. For example, the number 51 (*x*-axis) represents California. See Figure 3.3.7 (page 20) for the number of votes cast in the 2016 presidential election.

Chapter 5

The Electoral College Process

5.1 Description

According to Article II, Section 1, Clause 2 of the US Constitution, any state's number of electors equals the size of its total congressional delegation (i.e., House and Senate seats). After every decade, the slate of representatives is wiped clean and a completely new set of proportional numbers is calculated using the method of equal proportions.

///

The Electoral College follows a rigorous process of high integrity with checks and balances to elect a president and vice president of the United States. The 12th Amendment was ratified on June 15, 1804, which modified and clarified the election clause. The House of Representatives and the Senate controls the integrity of the process. For example, South Carolina gained one seat, up from six to seven, in its delegation because of the 2010 census. Therefore, it has seven representatives and two senators for a combined total delegation of nine in Congress. Consequently, a total of nine electors from South Carolina voted in the 2012 Electoral College and the same in the 2016 election. Another state lost a seat to maintain the limit of 435 House seats. See example—Tables 2.2.1, 2.2.2, and 2.2.3, pages 8–10.

///

In these analyses, the simple yet rigorous and powerful formula for reapportionment is an equitable approach in proportional reasoning to

5.1 Description, *cont.*

equalizing each state's representation in government. To that end, the Electoral College is fair and on solid ground. The total popular vote of the United States as one large integer, or number, is mathematically irrelevant to proportionality and fairness relative to the Electoral College and electing the president and vice president of the United States of America.

5.2 The 12th Amendment—US Constitution

This amendment outlines the Electoral College process. "The Electors shall meet in their respective states, and vote by ballot for President and Vice-President, one of whom, at least, shall not be an inhabitant of the same state with themselves; they shall name in their ballots the person voted for as President, and in distinct ballots the person voted for as Vice-President, and they shall make distinct lists of all persons voted for as President, and all persons voted for as Vice-President and of the number of votes for each, which lists they shall sign and certify, and transmit sealed to the seat of the government of the United States, directed to the President of the Senate;

The President of the Senate shall, in the presence of the Senate and House of Representatives, open all the certificates and the votes shall then be counted;

The person having the greatest Number of votes for President, shall be the President, if such number be a majority of the whole number of Electors appointed; and if no person has such majority, then from the persons having the highest numbers not exceeding three on the list of those voted for as President, the House of Representatives shall choose immediately, by ballot, the President. But in choosing the President, the votes shall be taken by states, the representation from each state having one vote; a quorum for this purpose shall consist of a member or members from two-thirds of the states, and a majority of all the states shall be necessary to a choice. And if the House of Representatives shall not choose a President whenever the right of choice shall devolve upon them, before the fourth day of March next following, then the Vice-President shall act as President, as in the case of the death or other constitutional disability of the President.

The person having the greatest number of votes as Vice-President, shall be the Vice-President, if such number be a majority of the whole number of Electors appointed, and if no person has a majority, then from the two highest numbers on the list, the Senate shall choose the Vice-President; a quorum for the purpose shall consist of two-thirds of the whole number

5.2 The 12th Amendment—US Constitution, *cont.*

of Senators, and a majority of the whole number shall be necessary to a choice. But no person constitutionally ineligible to the office of President shall be eligible to that of Vice-President of the United States."[1]

5.3 Flowchart—Electoral College Process

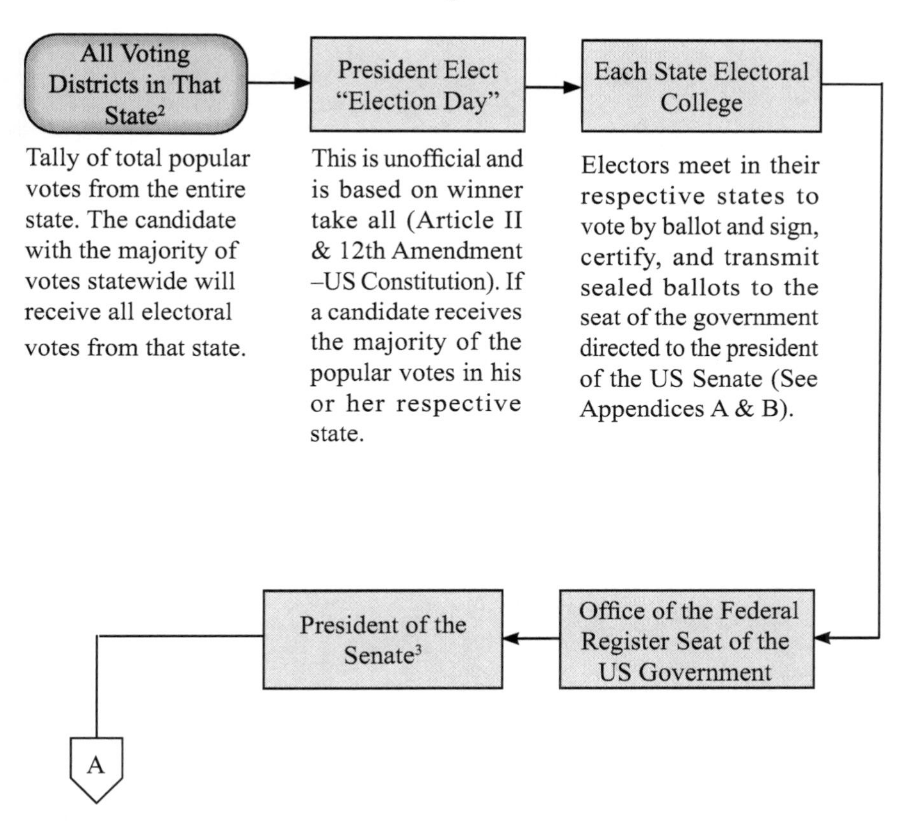

Figure 5.3.1: Flowchart—Electoral College Process (12th Amendment).

[1] Full text as written in the US Constitution.

[2] You cast your vote on election day.

[3] In the presence of the Senate and House of Representatives, the president of the Senate opens all the certificates and count the votes. (See Appendices A, B, and C).

5.3 Flowchart—Electoral College Process, *cont.*

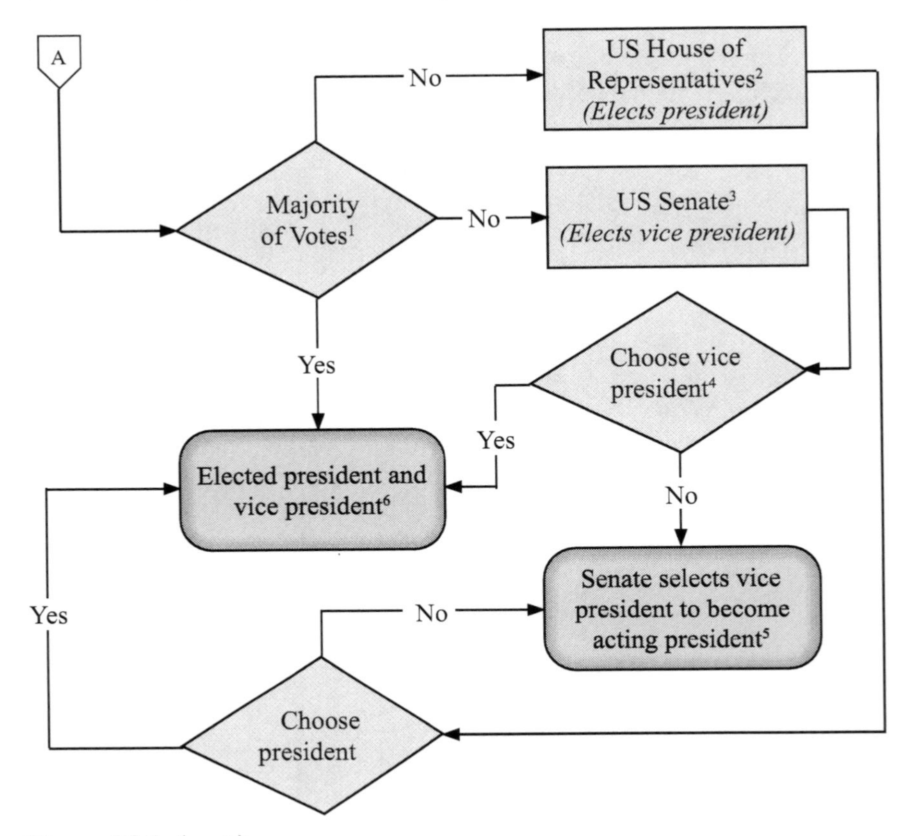

Figure 5.3.1: (cont.)

[1] In this decision path, the majority means 270 Electoral College votes out of 538 for the current presidential election. Also, yes or no for president and vice president.

[2] In this path, the House of Representatives would choose the president. Each state gets only one vote if the election is thrown into the House of Representatives. The last time a presidential election was thrown into the House of Representative was 1824.

[3] In this path, the Senate chooses the vice president from the majority of electors appointed.

[4] If no person is elected president, then the vice president is appointed acting president. If no person from the vice president list has a majority, then from the two highest numbers on the list, the Senate shall choose the vice president; a quorum for the purpose shall consist of two-thirds of the whole number of senators, and a majority of the whole numbers shall be necessary to the choice. But no person constitutionally ineligible to the office of president shall be eligible to that of vice president of the United States. The House will vote from a list of two candidates; the candidate with the highest number of electoral votes will become acting president (See 12th Amendment for more details).

[5] If a president is not elected, the vice president will act as president as in the case of death or other constitutional disability of the president. This person is now the president of the United States.

[6] Valid only if a president and vice president are elected.

Chapter 6

Summary

I have made every effort to convey to the public—using graphs, mathematics, and statistics—that proportionality and voting power are adequate and fair in the Electoral College process in electing the president and vice president of the United States of America. The United States is a republic and not a pure democracy. The founders who drafted the Constitution recognized this difference, which is clearly indicated in the US Constitution in Article IV, Section 4, where every state is guaranteed a republican form of government. Article II, Section 1 of the US Constitution is compatible with Article IV, Section 4. Therefore, electing the US president by popular vote would most likely undermine an equitable and practical proportional process of electing the president and vice president.

The information in this book proves that proportionality has been demonstrated. The regression analysis's R-squared values represent the proportional relationships (strength) among the sets of data, which have an average of about 99.5% fit and are an almost perfect fit between the population and apportionment as well as between the population and electors. Additionally, the chi-square test has a $p = 0.999$, which is an indication of strong equality in proportions among the popular vote, House seats, and electors. Equally important is that voting power is proportionate, and, without the Electoral College, there would not be a need for a candidate to put together a winning coalition from various states; hence, every state has a voice through the Electoral College. See Figure 3.3.6, page 19.

The analyses in this book also indicate that despite the vast differences between populous and less populous states, a voice is provided to every state on a proportional basis, whereas a popular vote would diminish or

Summary, *cont.*

completely silence the voice of the less populous states. Obviously, the larger states such as California have a more powerful voice than Wyoming. Nevertheless, the smaller states are still represented fairly based on their population. California is about 39% more populous than the next largest state, which is Texas. This gap makes the notion of a national popular vote unwise and threatens the 50 republican forms of government.

///

For example, in the 2016 presidential election, the candidate who won the states of California (14 million voted), New York (7.7 million voted), and Illinois (5.5 million voted) did so by a margin of 62.2 to 31.8%, 58.8 to 37.5%, and 58.5 to 38.8%, respectively. This is a spread of more than 20 percentage points in each of these three states, which is lopsided. The popular vote difference between the two major candidates in these three states was about 6.8 million votes. California alone accounted for 4.3 million of the 6.8 million vote spread. This is a situation where a few states could easily swing a victory for one candidate in a nationwide popular vote contest (Figure 3.3.7, page 20). Consequently, in a nation that is split about evenly between two political parties, it might not be unusual in the future for a candidate to win the popular vote but instead lose the electoral vote, and vice versa.

///

The states' population and electors are proportional in terms of the population, Electoral College, and voting power. Conversely, without the Electoral College method, smaller states would not have a voice. To that end, the total votes cast in a nationwide presidential election are inconsequential in the United States because of Article II–Section 1 and Article IV–Section 4 (US Constitution).

The idea is that the best result is achieved by the Electoral College process, which guarantees proportionate voting power compared to a popular vote, which provides little to no voting power for smaller states. Moreover, the operative word is that the Electoral College forces presidential candidates to put together a winning coalition, which can only be done in the current two-step process (Electoral College) that gives voice to all state voters.

In closing, let me say that I have endeavored mightily to assemble the pieces to show how the current system is a proportional and fair process for electing the US presidential and vice president. Therefore, it is my sincere hope and desire that this book will serve to answer many of the questions concerning the fairness and keeping the Electoral College. ■

List of References

Burnett, Kirstin. "Congressional Apportionment Quick Briefs 2010."
https://www.census.gov/prod/cen2010/briefs/c2010br-08.pdf

Croker, Royce. "The House of Representatives Apportionment Formula: An Analysis of Proposals for Change and Their Impact on States." 2010.
https://archives-democrats-rules.house.gov/Archives/RL31074

Huckabee, David C. "The House Apportionment Formula in Theory and Practice." 2000.
https://www.everycrsreport.com Report #RL3071

US Census Bureau.
"Apportionment of the US House of Representatives Based on the 2010 Census." 2010.
https://www.census.gov/population/apportionment/files/2010map.pdf.

US Census Bureau.
"Congressional Apportionment, Computing Apportionment." 2010.
https://www.census.gov/population/apportionment/about/

US National Archives and Records Administration
Office of the Federal Register. "US Electoral College Home Page."
https://www.archives.gov/federal-register/electoral-col
lege/roles.html. (accessed August 2018).

US National Archives and Record Administration, Office of the Federal Register. "US Electoral College—Presidential Election, Certificate of Attainment."
https://www.archives.gov/federal-register/electoral-col
lege/2016-certificates/pdfs/ascertainment-south-carolina.pdf.
(accessed August 2018).

U.S. Const. art. I, § 3

U.S. Const. art. II, § 1

U.S. Const. art. IV, § 4

U.S. Const. amend. XII

Appendix A

2012: State of South Carolina Certificate of Ascertainment—page 1 of 3

State of South Carolina
Office of the Governor

Nikki R. Haley
Governor

1205 Pendleton Street
Columbia 29201

CERTIFICATE OF ASCERTAINMENT

This is to Certify that a General Election for Presidential and Vice-Presidential Electors was held on November 6, 2012. The below candidates received the following votes as certified to this office by the Board of State Canvassers:

CONSTITUTION PARTY

PRESIDENT: VIRGIL GOOD
VICE PRESIDENT: JIM CLYMER

Tony Romo	4,765
Margot Romo	4,765
Darrell Wallace	4,765
David Arthur	4,765
Veronica Arthur	4,765
Bobby Woods	4,765
Erica Woods	4,765
Perry Simpson	4,765
David Whetsell	4,765

DEMOCRATIC PARTY

PRESIDENT: BARACK OBAMA
VICE PRESIDENT: JOE BIDEN

David Rison	865,941
Hugh Rogers	865,941
Diane Anderson	865,941
Ron Ramine	865,941
Hattie Ross	865,941
Annejanet Harp	865,941
Cedric Spain	865,941
Dick Harpootlian	865,941
Melissa Watson	865,941

Figure A.1.1: Certificate of Ascertainment.[1]

[1] Source: US National Archives and Records Administration.

Appendix A, *cont.*

2012: State of South Carolina Certificate of Ascertainment—page 2 of 3

GREEN PARTY

PRESIDENT:	JILL STEIN
VICE PRESIDENT:	CHERI HONKALA
Earline Evans	5,446
William P. Kreml	5,446
J. David Gillespie	5,446
Vincent D. D'Amato	5,446
Eugene Platt	5,446
Jeanne vanden Hurk	5,446
Sue Edward	5,446
Gregg Jocoy	5,446
David Whiteman	5,446

LIBERTARIAN PARTY

PRESIDENT:	GARY JOHNSON
VICE PRESIDENT:	JAMES P. GRAY
Keith Blandford	16,321
F. John Perna	16,321
Michael Carmany	16,321
Laird Minor	16,321
Jennifer Shulz	16,321
Stewart Flood	16,321
Tristan Howard	16,321
Arch Wakefield	16,321
David Morris	16,321

Figure A.1.1: Certificate of Ascertainment, cont.[1]

[1] Source: US National Archives and Records Administration.

Appendix A, *cont.*

2012: State of South Carolina Certificate of Ascertainment—page 3 of 3

REPUBLICAN PARTY

PRESIDENT:	MITT ROMNEY
VICE PRESIDENT:	PAUL RYAN
Bruce Chadwick Connelly	1,071,645
Drew McKissick	1,071,645
Cynthia F. Costa	1,071,645
Randall S. Page	1,071,645
Janice C. McCord	1,071,645
Betty Sheppard Poe	1,071,645
Sandra R. Stroman	1,071,645
Roy Rex Lindsey III	1,071,645
James Edward Jerow	1,071,645

Witness, Her Excellency our Governor, Nikki R. Haley, and our seal hereto affixed in Columbia South Carolina this seventh day of December, in the year of our Lord, 2012.

NIKKI R. HALEY
Governor

MARK HAMMOND
SECRETARY OF STATE

Figure A.1.1: Certificate of Ascertainment, *cont.*[1]

[1] Source: US National Archives and Records Administration.

Appendix B

2012: State of South Carolina Certificate of Vote

The State of South Carolina

Office of Secretary of State Mark Hammond

2012 ELECTORAL COLLEGE CERTIFICATE OF VOTE

We, the undersigned, being duly elected Electors for President and Vice President of the United States, for the State of South Carolina, at the General Election held on Tuesday, November 6th, 2012, pursuant to the Constitution and laws of the United States and of this State, certify that the following candidates for President and Vice President received the following number of votes, by ballot, at the meeting of Electors held on Monday, December 17th, 2012, in Columbia, South Carolina.

FOR PRESIDENT OF THE UNITED STATES: MITT ROMNEY
NUMBER OF ELECTOR VOTES: 9

FOR VICE PRESIDENT OF THE UNITED STATES: PAUL RYAN
NUMBER OF ELECTOR VOTES: 9

BRUCE CHADWICK CONNELLY (AT-LARGE)

DREW MCKISSICK (AT-LARGE)

CYNTHIA L. [illegible] (1ST CONG. DIST.)

RANDALL S. PAGE (2ND CONG. DIST.)

JANICE C. MCCORD (3RD CONG. DIST.)

BETTY SHEPPARD POE (4TH CONG. DIST.)

SANDRA R. STROMAN (5TH CONG. DIST.)

ROY RE[illegible] LINDSEY, III (6TH CONG. DIST.)

JAMES EDWARD JEROW (7TH CONG. DIST.)

ALTERNATE

ALTERNATE

In Testimony whereof, I have hereunto set my hand and affixed the Great Seal of the State of South Carolina at the State Capitol in the City of Columbia, South Carolina, on this seventeenth day of December, 2012.

Mark Hammond, Secretary of State

Figure B.1.1: Certificate of Vote.[1]

[1] Source: US National Archives and Records Administration.

Appendix C

Table C.1.1: Listed as Table 1for this report.[1] Apportionment Population of the US House of Representatives—2010.

U.S. Department of Commerce
U.S. Census Bureau

Table 1. APPORTIONMENT POPULATION AND NUMBER OF REPRESENTATIVES, BY STATE: 2010 CENSUS

STATE	APPORTIONMENT POPULATION (APRIL 1, 2010)	NUMBER OF APPORTIONED REPRESENTATIVES BASED ON 2010 CENSUS	CHANGE IN SEATS FROM CENSUS 2000 APPORTIONMENT
Alabama	4,802,982	7	0
Alaska	721,523	1	0
Arizona	6,412,700	9	+1
Arkansas	2,926,229	4	0
California	37,341,989	53	0
Colorado	5,044,930	7	0
Connecticut	3,581,628	5	0
Delaware	900,877	1	0
Florida	18,900,773	27	+2
Georgia	9,727,566	14	+1
Hawaii	1,366,862	2	0
Idaho	1,573,499	2	0
Illinois	12,864,380	18	-1
Indiana	6,501,582	9	0
Iowa	3,053,787	4	-1
Kansas	2,863,813	4	0
Kentucky	4,350,606	6	0
Louisiana	4,553,962	6	-1
Maine	1,333,074	2	0
Maryland	5,789,929	8	0
Massachusetts	6,559,644	9	-1
Michigan	9,911,626	14	-1
Minnesota	5,314,879	8	0
Mississippi	2,978,240	4	0
Missouri	6,011,478	8	-1
Montana	994,416	1	0
Nebraska	1,831,825	3	0
Nevada	2,709,432	4	+1
New Hampshire	1,321,445	2	0
New Jersey	8,807,501	12	-1
New Mexico	2,067,273	3	0
New York	19,421,055	27	-2
North Carolina	9,565,781	13	0
North Dakota	675,905	1	0
Ohio	11,568,495	16	-2
Oklahoma	3,764,882	5	0
Oregon	3,848,606	5	0
Pennsylvania	12,734,905	18	-1
Rhode Island	1,055,247	2	0
South Carolina	4,645,975	7	+1
South Dakota	819,761	1	0
Tennessee	6,375,431	9	0
Texas	25,268,418	36	+4
Utah	2,770,765	4	+1
Vermont	630,337	1	0
Virginia	8,037,736	11	0
Washington	6,753,369	10	+1
West Virginia	1,859,815	3	0
Wisconsin	5,698,230	8	0
Wyoming	568,300	1	0
TOTAL[1]	309,183,463	435	

[1]Apportionment population includes the resident population for the 50 states, as ascertained by the Twenty-Third Decennial Census under Title 13, United States Code, and counts of overseas U.S. military and federal civilian employees (and their dependents living with them) allocated to their home state, as reported by the employing federal agencies. The apportionment population excludes the population of the District of Columbia.

The above table was borrowed from Congressional Apportionment—2010 Census Briefs.

About the Author

David C. Wilson is an electrical engineer by training as well as an adjunct statistics and mathematics professor—now retired. He is a statistical consultant, local historian, author, and self-publisher.

He has had a keen interest since high school in voting patterns, political elections, and the role played by each branch of government at the national, state, and local levels. During his teenage years, Dave encouraged and cajoled others to register to vote during a challenging time in southern voting history. In addition, he has read and studied the US Constitution, including the Electoral College process extensively over the years.

Dave has published two family history books and his high school alumni book, covering graduating classes from 1955 to 1970. He researched and published papers on local history; public school student performance trends at the national, state, and district levels; and science, technology, engineering, and mathematics (STEM) worker trends.

He served three years in the US Army, and, after his military service, he earned his bachelor's degree from the City College of New York, followed by a master's degree in electrical engineering from Manhattan College (New York).

Thereafter, during his career, Dave worked for IBM, General Electric, and Honeywell. He also taught as an adjunct mathematics professor at Dutchess Community College, Quinnipiac University, and Horry-Georgetown Technical College for more than 25 years. Along the way, he tutored middle and high school students for more than 30 years in mathematics and science.
With industry and academic experience spanning three decades, he retired to found and lead Wilson Consulting Services, LLC.

Dave and his wife, Beverly, live in South Carolina and spend time with their grandchildren, two sons, and their families.

Institutions—US Government

Capitol Building—US Congress
Established under Article I, US Constitution

White House—The President
Established under Article II, US Constitution

US Supreme Court Building—Supreme Court Justices
Established under Article III, US Constitution

Made in the USA
Columbia, SC
14 August 2024

40455932R10030